From My World to Yours
Poems from the soul about everyday life

Volume I

This is for Ya'll

From My World to Yours
Poems from the soul about everyday life
Volume I

Written by:
Bob Baker

Photography:
Jill Baker

—

Thank You to Jill Baker, my wife and best friend, for all of the photography and shared love for traveling the back roads where I get my inspiration.

Table of Contents

Preface

I truly hope you find enjoyment from my poems. I consider each more than a poem and more a story in itself. The things that give me inspiration vary from a true life experience to something I see on the side of the road. As we all travel through life we encounter happiness and sorrow but through each we become a stronger wiser person. We all go through the same good times and rough times in life and hopefully a page in this book whether a poem or a photo will be just what you need at that time to help you through. So live your life to the fullest and understand that our life path is already in place and just waiting for us to take the next step.

Listening to the Morning Rain

There is nothing more relaxing than the sound of a
summer morning rain
If your are sad, hurting or missing someone it seems
to take away the pain

I was reflecting and remembering back at some of the
best times of my youth
And they were times laughing and talking with
friends as rain fell on the roof

The air that comes to us with the rain is all so fresh
and new
Especially mixed with the morning mist between the
rain and dew

As I sit on the porch rocking with a cup of steaming
coffee in my hand
I look over the meadow with morning rain and breeze
of the ceiling fan

To me there is nothing quite so relaxing on our little
dead end lane
Than to sit and rock with my bride just listening to
the morning rain

Preaching With the Serpent (SNAKES)

Sunday while driving in eastern Kentucky
I was down in the dumps when I got lucky

There on my left was a little country church
With a bunch of cars and trucks all covered in dirt

Then I said to myself this looks like a great place
I'll find me a seat in a pew that has extra space

Then the preacher took the stage and he began to roar
About how we're sinners and will burn in hell ever
more

He then picked up a bucket and swung it at the crowd
And people started chanting and all crying out loud

There were snakes all flying across those church pews
I'm not sure how many but I guarantee a 100 or two

A lady caught one flying at us and thank God she did
not miss
Then looked straight at it in the eyes and gave it a big
ole kiss

I decided it was time to go and run toward the door
But when I looked down snakes were all over the
floor

continued

My legs began to tremble and I had nowhere to run
But I knew I had to get out of there cause kissing
snakes ain't fun

I jumped from pew to pew until at last I was out the
door
I can say without a doubt I ain't going to that snake
church no more

A Fathers Gift to You

When you grow old and your hair turns grey
I hope you will look at my picture and say

My Dad was one whose love never failed
He was there for me and he never bailed

He was the one that all throughout my days
Was always there even when he had hard things to
say

The hard lessons about life sometimes hurt but are
true
Sometimes they are words that you need said to you

Then there were days when I felt alone in this world
My Dad always had that sense and was there in a
whirl

A true loving Father's job is not to be your best friend
But a role model, mentor and Your Safety net until
the very end

Little Country Church

It sits proudly in the corn field on the hill there all
alone
With shutters hanging and paint peeling its years are
surely shown

Beside her and behind that broken and faded old
white picket fence
Old time family members were placed so their after
life could commence

The grounds are now ragged and covered with years
of growth
For the youngsters they all grew up and moved away
years ago

There are no families living out in this countryside
anymore
No more church bells ringing or folks seeking shelter
in a storm

Where there once were church socials with Martha's
famous pie
Now the church hall sits empty and the wind sounds
like it cries

The church pews are broken and dusty and falling on
the floor
For in it's soul it knows there will never be sermons
like before

continued

There will be no more singing or Easter Egg hunts in the yard
Yes, looking at this Little Country Church that is falling down is very hard

Day We Fear May Be Very Near

This ordinary beautiful autumn day started just like
every other
I was doing my business and it was the birthday of
my mother

I will never forget how in an instant my life changed
that day
As I sat in disbelief listening to what the Dr. had to
say

He told me things were dreadful with not a moment
left to spare
I will never forget how blue the sky was as I walked
out of there

I sat in the car there all alone and just pondered over
things in my life
Just thinking what was going to happen to my
daughter and my wife

The hardest thing I ever did was to sit there and give
them the news
To tell them what the Dr said and the choices from
which to choose

I made the choice that day I would fight this battle
and refuse to loose
And I would be there for my daughter's graduation no
matter what I had to do

-continued

My daughter's graduation day has long since come
and gone
But I still fight my battle in my mind and I will from
now on

We each have our battles in life that we fight each
and every day
But as we fight these wars in life we get stronger in
our own way

So when you get up today and think your life plans
are clear
Always remember that the day you fear may be very
near

The Hurt

We have all had times when we were let down
Times when we cried and times when we frowned

These acts that hurt us sometimes were thought
through and planned
While other times they unwittingly happened just like
blowing sand

Sometimes these hurts are done by someone that we
love
And other times hurt comes from a person we hardly
knew of

The hurt that's the worst doesn't come from a gun or
a fist
It's the ones that attack your heart that are hardest to
resist

These heartbreaking hurts go through you like a
dagger's hard thrust
And leave you with empty feelings of helplessness
and no trust

So as you go through your life and not giving it much
thought
Remember what you say to another just may affect
them a whole lot

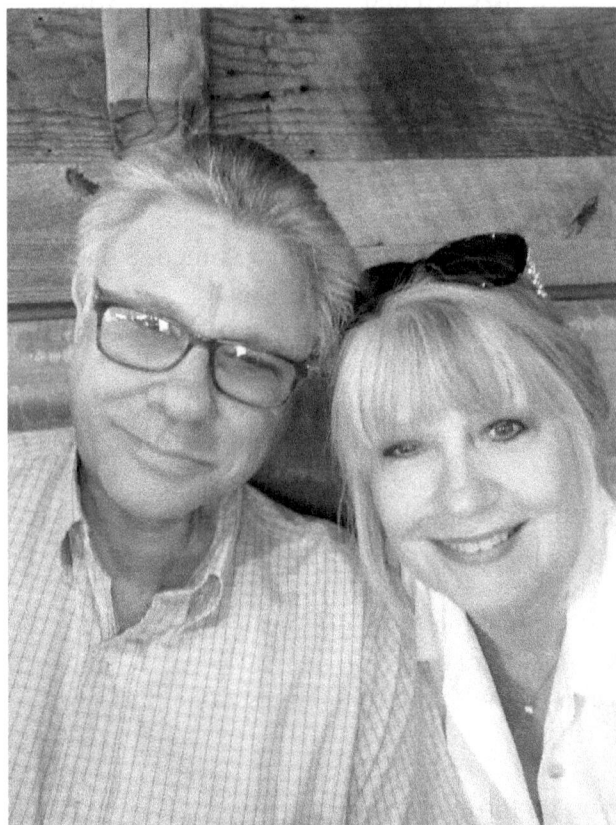

Through Sadness and Fun

Through all of these years that we've been together
And all the ups and downs together we have
weathered

The one thing that has always been there for sure
Is that no matter what happened our love would
endure

Many Birthdays for us both have since come and
gone
And yet through them all we manage to still carry on

The true test of one's love is not through laughter and
smiles
But sustaining that love through life's turmoil and
trials

Looking back my life has been good this is true
And a big part of the reason is it was with you

So as you set out on your next trip around the sun
I'll be there with you through the sadness and fun

Burying Our Friend

Years ago we all came together to celebrate our
wedding days
There was laughter and rejoicing telling stories of our
single ways

The next time we got together it seems it is bury
someone's Mom or Dad
The conversations were a lot more subtle and stories
seemed a little sad

Then we all got together again for our 40 year reunion
and had lots of fun
Where we laughed and talked about our retirement,
wives, daughters and sons

Then it seems too soon it happens and some lives are
gone like the wind
And now we all get together again but sadly this time
it's to Bury Our Friend

Front Porch

There was a time in our past and it wasn't too long
ago
When everyone on the street were people that you
know

As you walked down the street you waved and said hi
They asked where you were going as you slowly
drove by

Mrs. Brown was always sitting and shelling her peas
With her stockings rolled down just below her knees

We all knew what was happening anywhere in the
town
For neighbors would always stop to spread the gossip
all around

You knew who was having a baby and who got fired
from their job
You knew who was sneaking out drinking and who
was a snob

We all looked out for our neighbors and them we all
knew
And they returned the favor always looking out for
you

Sadly this kind of life burned out like a torch
As America quit building houses with a front porch

True or Not- Do You Really Know

Have you ever wondered about all the things that we hear and see
Just how much of the information is true that's told to you and me

We hear stories from news, advertising and even from our friends
Then there is the gossip that goes flying around every now and then

A boy when dating will make up a crazy excuse to tell his girlfriend
She turns around with something just as crazy that she tells to him

The government only tells you and I just what they want us to know
Husbands and wives cheating on each other tell lies that continue to grow

Then there are all of the children that don't tell their parents the truth
These childhood lies are told by kids though out teen years and youth

If we only knew everything was the truth it would be something to bestow
But since we don't just ask yourself - True or Not- do you really know

---

Smell of a Brand New Car

While at the car dealer following my wife's bad luck

I decide to walk over and sit my ass in a brand new truck

Then all of a sudden it hit me just like a ton of brick

Something you and I can't duplicate and I did not predict

It attacked my brain just as though I was craving an addictive drug

I couldn't resist and no matter how I tried I couldn't pull the plug

I fought the urge with everything inch of strength that I had

It was like a conspiracy or like I was possessed it was just that bad

I gave into the urge and sprinted onto that showroom floor

I tried my very best but I just couldn't fight it anymore

continued

Scientists have tried to recreate this smell over the world near and far

But no one has been able to duplicate the SMELL OF A BRAND NEW CAR

Good Old Days

Forty Five years have just come and gone it seems
like way to fast
It seems like only yesterday that we were laughing
and cutting up in class

Some of us now no longer work and are just living
our life as planned
While others have been fighting problems more than
most of us could stand

Some of us have fought illness and watched loved
ones not make it through
While others spent their time working out in the gym
maybe even took Kung Fu

Some of us like to camp and enjoy life in the great
outdoors
While others like to spend their time at the mall
shopping in the stores

I loved to see the smiles on faces that through life
have never died
We talked about stupid things we did and I laughed
until I cried

It seems we have all gone on with our lives and
drifted different ways
But when we got together it still seemed like the
GOOD OLD DAYS

—

If It Could Only Last Forever

Christmas when Santa brought you that brand new
bike
Gazing through the bakery counter picking what you
like

Going out on that first date with the one you love
Or the day your child was baptized accepting the
Lord above

It could be your high school graduation or your
Senior Prom
Maybe just sitting on the front porch talking with
your Mom

Was it your wedding day or the day your child was
born
It might be for you the first night spent in your
college dorm

We all have in our past, these special times that stand
out
They come and go in an instant but affect our life no
doubt

They are upon us then they're gone like the wind
blows away a feather
And we are just left standing there wishing if this
could only last forever

Facebook It Must Be True

While eating my lunch today I was looking at my
phone
I wasn't reading news or email I was in that Facebook
zone

What has happened to people and the way that we
tend to think
When we can't put our phone and Facebook down
even while we eat

You look around a restaurant and everyone's the
same
They are no longer talking with each other and that's
a total shame

You see people driving down the road not looking out
ahead
Because they are busy checking Facebook to see what
someone said

I believe for Facebook some people would sell their
very soul
Like an addiction in their life Facebook has taken
complete control

Then you have the people that devourer every
Facebook post
And totally ignore people and things in live that really
matter most

Continued

It seems we all know people that are friends of me and you
That sadly live life thinking if it's on Facebook it must be true

True Love Starts

I know some people believe love begins there at first
sight
For others they think it's during a slow dance in soft
dim light

Some couples feel the love begins at a time unknown
to them
And there are couples that feel the love at their first
date's end

These times for true love to start sound romantic and
very sweet
But the truth of the matter is that the time it begins is
not quite so neat

What hits us on the dance floor or on that first date is
not true love
Just as real true love doesn't fall upon us from the
stars up above

What starts with infatuation slowly grows into a
deeper bond
Then through life's trials and tribulations it continues
to build upon

But when your love is dying or suffering and it's
tearing apart your heart
Then and only then my friend is when undying deep
true love starts

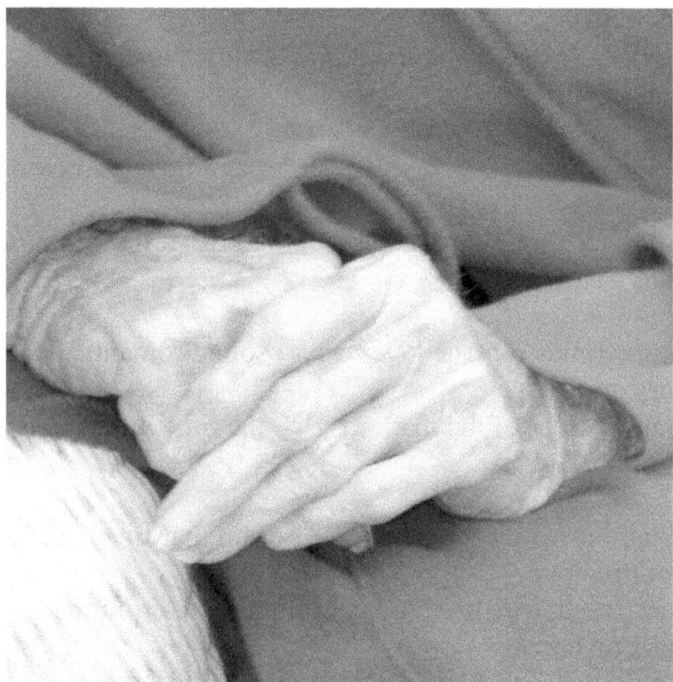

Last Words from Me

When a loved one leaves and walks out the door
Maybe they go to work or maybe go to the store

It might be a child has grown up and is moving away
Or maybe someone we love is just going out for the
day

How many times has someone left without words
being said
Even while we will never know what in life lies ahead

It might be the last time that we see them for all that
we know
So we need to tell them we love them every time that
they go

I want my loved ones to know that if life ends for me
after you leave
I want you to remember I LOVE YOU as the last
words from me

Growing Up In My Small Town

Life was simple and the times they were fun
Summer days in the lake to beat the heat and sun

In cut off blue jeans and no shoes were ever worn
We would just use our knife if we stepped on a thorn

Saturdays we all rode downtown on our Shwinn bikes
Eating ice cream and watching a movie that we all
liked

After supper kids washed dishes and watched TV
together
With only 3 channels to choose we just had to watch
whatever

Curfew by parents when out on a date Saturday Night
Were firmly set without exception for the stroke of
midnight

No stores open Wednesday afternoon or Sunday at
the time
And nowhere on Sunday could you ever buy beer or
wine

Friday night football games were the event of the
week
To all of us kids the players were true heroes I think

The parents they knew all of the kids that were
coming around
Yes life sure was great growing up in my small town

Surely Miss This All

I was thinking about the life that the kids live today
With video games, cell phones and not going out to
play

They have no reason anymore to hang on the phone
The way we did for hours when our parents were not
at home

If they want to breakup with a girl they just send her a
short text
They don't even talk about whose fault it was or what
they do next

They don't run out of gas and have their friends push
the car home
Now they just call Mom and Dad's motor club on
their I- phone

They don't know what it's like to work a job each day
after school
And earn their own money to pay for their own car
and their fuel

They will never know the joy of an having an RC and
Moon Pie
Now they go to McDonalds drive thru for a Latte and
some fries

continued

They have no school pride or spirit it seems like
anymore
The way we did on Friday nights at dances on the
gym floor

They don't ride their bikes in the mud and get dirty
and all wet
Because Mom's today are afraid of them getting
germs and get all upset

We could not wait for summer and for school again in
the fall
Now with kids just being home schooled they will
surely miss this all

May Be Your Last

Have you ever wondered just how long you will be on
this earth
And when you are gone what your life will have
really been worth

There will be people that remember the good times
with you
Maybe some will have memories of a love that was
deep and true

Then there may be others that say thank goodness that
you are gone
There are others that have no interest in you and their
life just moves along

One thing is for certain in life and this we can not
deny
And that is that one day it will happen and we will all
die

That time may come for you today, next week or
maybe come next year
So just live your life to the fullest and death is not to
fear

So don't waste time worrying about things that
happened in your past
And live each day to the fullest for today may very
well be your last

Fit like a Glove

When you meet someone with whom you want to
share and live your life
There are certain things you need to know so not to
cause a lot of strife

You need to understand that each of you have a
different view
So don't try to change each other into something that
suits you

You have to accept the things about them that maybe
you don't like
Just because you join lives doesn't mean you need to
be just alike

You may like jeans and boots and listening to a
country song
And they like wine and dresses and show tunes that
they sing along

You want to eat BBQ and beer while sitting in a local
bar
Where they prefer Champaign and snacking on
Russian caviar

So accept all of the things about that special someone
that you love
And understand you will never fit each other like a
fine custom glove

Only In The USA

They think it proves something by not standing in
honor of our flag

But this type of behavior does nothing but make a
decent person gag

They say that the country is treating them wrong and
things they must change

But it's not the country's fault families have become
dysfunctional and estranged

You have kids out in the world with no father that
they will ever know

They have mothers that do not care where they are or
where at night they go

They roam the streets without supervision which only
leads down a path of no return

So they end up with the wrong group that teach them
to rob, steal and burn

They go through youth with no guidance and have
nowhere to turn

Which leads to a life of crime or public assistance
because that's all they've learned

continued

Before you blame our country for all of your disappointments and your woes

Take a look in the mirror and the real reason for your problems will surely show

So quit blaming society for your bad decisions is all I have to say

Because the truth is you can become what you choose only in the USA

Walmart on Saturday Night

Some come by car some come by truck and some
even come by bus
If they think you got their parking spot they flick you
off and cuss

Some are dressed in Sunday best while others do not
care
Maybe its pajamas and bedroom slippers some even
choose to wear

They get a new battery for the car and a brand new
kitchen rug
Then pick up toys for the kids and Grandma's
prescription drugs

While they shop they get their taxes done and glasses
with new frames
And some of the kids hang out at the door playing the
arcade games

There is something there for everyone no matter what
you like
Whether it's watches, guns, hamburger meat or
maybe a new bike

When I go there it's always fun to watch the people
and the sites
I swear there is no better place to go than Walmart on
Saturday night

Love you.
mom & Dad.

My Grandpa

His hair was full and as white as new fallen snow
Wearing a white starched shirt everywhere he'd go

Fedora in wool for the winter and straw for summer
So distinguished why we adored him was no wonder

In his car we would load and go to ride for the day
On a back country road he'd find a creek for us to
play

Us kids in our underwear in the creek we would
splash
Swinging from a rope in a tree into the water we'd
crash

Upon getting home in Grandma's big bed we would
pile
Soon all would drift away into dreams with big smiles

Grandpa always said don't spend your life working
for gold
When family not money brings happiness to your soul

He said do not spend your life indebted to any other
man
Time with family not possessions will keep you
happy as you can

continued

Without these strong family values who knows where
I might be
Thank you Grandpa for teaching your values to my
siblings, cousins and me

Hurricane Weatherman

The big blow is now on the radar and it's heading our way
TV news only talking hurricane stuff and nothing more today

There is always one way to tell how bad things out there really are
And it is not determined by studying the moon the sun or radar

The only sure way to tell how bad the weather is to become
Is by the stage of the shirt tie and suit worn on TV by some

You can tell how bad things are getting by the weatherman's clothes
As weather gets bad why their wardrobe changes nobody knows

It all starts slow as you see them all removing their suit coat
Then as things begin to get worse they loosen their tie from their throat

The next step of the weatherman shirt plan is when things really get bad
Their sleeves are rolled up and wrinkled and they look fighting mad

continued

You don't have to even hear them saying when to
execute your storm plan
You just need to check time to time on the shirt status
of the hurricane weatherman

Lessons of Love

Life always works in such mysterious ways
As things will change contiguously day to day

The only thing constant and seems to drop from above
Are the things we learn in life thru the lessons of love

We learn thru the lessons of love there is more than ourselves
As we have to put our own interests away on the back shelf

We let our heart venture to new places unknown
Fore when in this new love your are no longer alone

We will have days when things are bad and some that are fun
But they are all days to cherish because of this special one

There are times when this love will be put to the test
But you will get through it fore your partner's the best

You will not reflect on the anger and sorrow and such
But you will surely reflect on the one you love oh so very much

When you look back and remember the great times in your mind

continued

Chances are love played a big part in this memory
you'll find

At the end of your life as you are lying there and
beginning to die
You won't remember bad but the good times and love
of your life

Eventually Fade Away

We all come into this world needing help with every
need
The things in life are learned by all but at a different
speed

As we go through our youth it seems like our life will
never end
But some will die young and why this is so is hard to
comprehend

Some of us will leave this world from violence or an
act of war
While others will just fade away to sleep and wake
nevermore

There are those of us that will have to watch while
our children die
For others they will watch their Mom and Dad fade
and gently cry

The thought of death is something from which we all
seem to hide
But the reality is that we will all be there and this can
not be denied

So as you go through life be sure to love your family
each and everyday
Because it is certain that one day the lives of us all
will eventually fade away

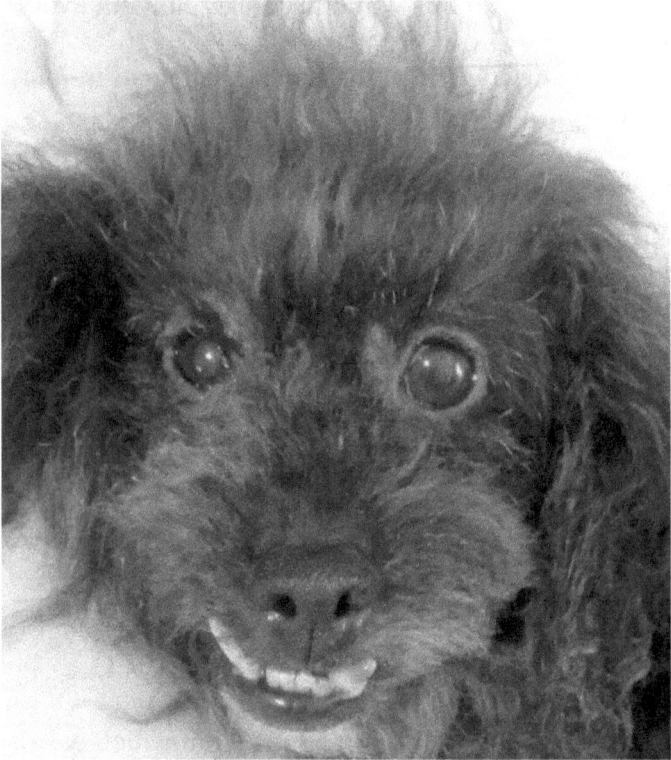

Little Buddy and Me

He lays there on the couch with me just as close as he
can get
Then the door bell rings and he is off to the door just
like a flying jet

Back to his perch where he watches squirrels play
through the glass back door
His little cloudy eyes are gazing around but don't see
that well anymore

His little teeth have never been quite straight as they
should be
The missing hair that comes and goes is such a
mystery to me

During days of his younger life he was our daughter's
precious pet
He would play in dress up clothes and sleep with her
from the day they first met

Our daughter is now all grown up and from our home
had to move away
So our little buddy is content with his mom and I with
him everyday

He has a little separation issue that when he can't see
you he begins to cry
But when you step back in the room he looks at you
and lets out a loving sigh

-continued

He can no longer jump up on the bed or couch and is getting older I can see
But he still loves his Sunday Dairy Queen ride with Mom, Little Buddy and Me

Worst Days of My Life

Every morning when I wake up from a good night sleep
A new day begins with new memories that I will forever keep

There are days in my life some are fun and some are truly great
And then there are the days I live that we all just have to hate

I looked back at my life and my worst days and there were four
These are the days that as long as I live in my mind I will store

We all have these days that we wished never were there
But we will all have memories of these days we shall bear

But with all of the great times I've had with my family, daughter and wife
I would never appreciate the best days if not for the worst days of my life

July 4th- America's Day

4th of July is upon us Americans to celebrate once
again
Most just see as day off work and don't know how it
began

It is recognizing the day when our Independence was
won
When we stood up with arms and defeated the
stronger one

We were tired of oppression; harsh ruling and taxes
So patriots came together fighting with guns, knives
and axes

We proved to the world that Americans were fierce
and we were strong
And if you want your freedom bad enough you must
fight what is wrong

This should stand as a lesson to the people in the
world oppressed today
That if you really want your freedom you must fight
and not run away

If you are willing to fight like America the greatest
country of them all
And you stand up fight and are willing to die the
tyrant only then will fall

The Declaration of Independence was signed on July
4, 1776
We have been together and apart at times throughout
history since

-continued

But one thing is for sure throughout the world far and wide
When America is tested it will not roll over or just lay down and die

So let it be known to the evil and terrorist blowing around like the wind
You don't want to take on America for we will fight until the very end

GOD BLESS AMERICA

This Morning

As I drink my coffee and wait for the sun to rise on
this new day
And quietly read through the news seeing what they
have to say

It's really very dishearten there is nothing at all good
to read
Just bickering about politics and statues nothing we
really need

It seems like with things in the world in such a
screwed up mess
The news really could find something more
worthwhile to address

There is turmoil in foreign countries and starvation in
other lands
Threats of nuclear war upon us just riding in a
lunatic's hands

Taxes are high and climbing to the point of no return
But no one cares to discuss this as if it's of no
concern

But the things that drive a fit of anger in the unstable
and insecure
You can bet will be on the front page of the news you
can rest assured

continued

So if you want to have a nice day, be in a good mood and not be so depressed
Just turn off the news and crank up the music in the morning as you get dressed

When the Little One Had to Leave

You wake up one morning with a new member in the
house
Until this time came upon you it was just you and
your spouse

Your life changed dramatically on that exciting day
For the next many years this young thing was there to
stay

Then all of a sudden one day things begin to change
When your most prized possession had to leave the
range

They are grown up now and you know that you did
all you could
But still you sadly watch while they walk out the door
for good

You know down in your heart it is time for them to go
And you try your very best for your sadness not to
show

As they leave you and move to the next step of their
life
You will never stop missing them no matter how you
try

On this hardest day of your life while you find it hard
to breathe
You find yourself so proud but so sad that your little
one had to leave

———

This Old House Was Spared

As I drove through my old neighborhood just the
other day
I stopped in the road and couldn't seem to look away

What I was looking at was more than shingles paint
and wood
It was memories of my family and these memories
there are good

This was the house where I lived throughout my
youthful years
It was a place of peace and comfort and where I even
shed a few tears

We would run and play with friends that lived around
our red clay street
And at night climb into bed with our windows open
while we went to sleep

Supper time we all ate at the kitchen table and talked
about our day
Momma took turns to listen to what each of us had to
say

We all did our part with dishes and cleaning up from
supper time
Not helping with the dishes in our house to Momma
was a crime

- continued

We all had our chores to do and school was a major responsibility
Our Momma insisted that everything be done to your best ability

I sat there remembering the good times this old house has shared
I'm thankful that though years and growth this old house has been spared

That Smile

Some people seem to find this little thing so very hard
to do
While others it just comes naturally whenever they
look at you

Some people wake in the morning with this all over
their face
There are others that wake like they are mad at the
whole human race

I had a man tell one time it is much easier to be happy
than to be sad
Maybe that's why when I wake up I'm always
whistling and I am glad

I try my best to laugh a lot and just take life as it
comes
Because sometimes we get the cake and sometimes
just the crumbs

A person's true beauty doesn't come from their looks
or their fashion style
But it comes from them sharing a lot of laughter and a
radiant beautiful smile

The Day We Lost Dad

Most of the time our days go through just like the last
But we all have days that were much different in our
past

Some of those days were fun and full of cheer
While others in our life were full of sadness or fear

What must have gone though the mind of my Mother
When she lived through a terrifying day like no other

That was the day she was told my father was dead
She had to have been terrified of what lied ahead

She was only a young mother with six kids to feed
How would she provide for the things six kids need

She thought her life through and put aside the sorrow
she felt
And said I must get to work and play the cards I was
dealt

My Mom she was fighter and refused to ever quit
Raising six small children while never complaining
one bit

She took sorrow that would have devastated most I
am glad
And became a true hero and fighter the day we lost
Dad

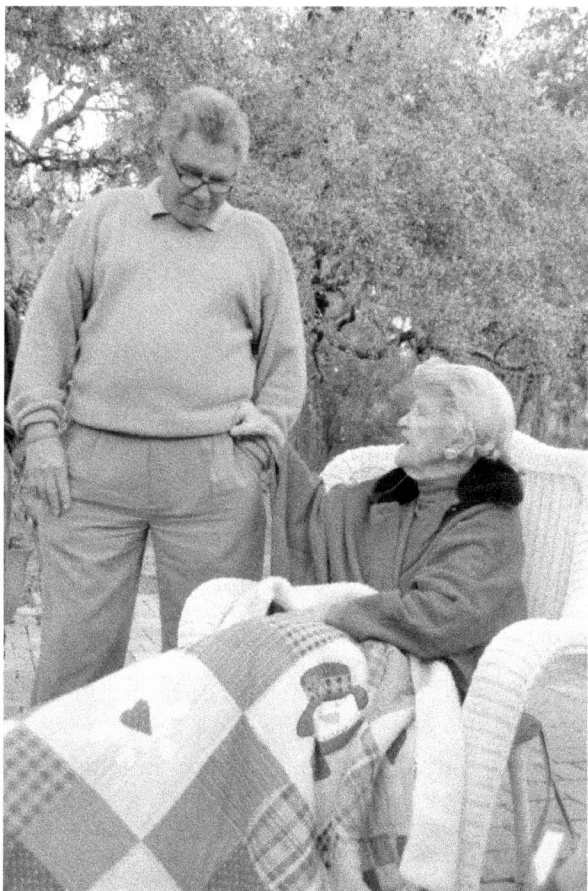

If Only For A Day

If you found a Jeannie in a bottle washed up on the
shore today
Then the Jeannie asked what you wanted, what is it
you would say

Would you ask for a million dollars or maybe a brand
new car
Maybe it would be a ride into space and visit a distant
star

For me it would be something simple and not cost a
single dime
It would be a day on the porch talking with Momma
just one more time

We could talk about the traffic or how the market has
climbed
Maybe she would tell me about the new recipe for her
pecan pie

Then she would tell me about what Dr. Phil said to
folks today
And then we would talk about the neighbors and who
passed away

She would then go to the kitchen and open her fully
stocked freezer door
Saying take this fish home for supper and you won't
need to stop at the store

- Continued

———

No my wish from a Jeannie wouldn't be for money or penthouse with a valet
It would be sitting in a rocking chair with Momma on the porch if only for a day

Respect for Each Other

You never seem to see a man anymore get up and
offer a lady his chair
Or remove their hat inside it's like they are afraid to
show their hair

It seems people will no longer take time to hold open
a door
And it is unusual to even hear someone say thank you
anymore

People just don't seem to care about showing each
other respect
Some of you may even take offense at me talking so
direct

Today a woman at the store just let the door shut in
my face
She was heading for a fountain drink like she was
running in a race

Whether it is showing a little courtesy in public or
while driving in your car
You may find out you like being courteous and it's
more rewarding by far

If people out there treated everyone like they were a
sister or brother
It would be such a better world full of courtesy and
respect for each other

The Love fades Away

There they are standing across that lightly lit room
You can't resist the draw as their eyes gaze at you

Your lives go from separate lives and then they
become one
Times are spent sharing love with days and nights of
fun

You have the joy of bringing into the world new life
With years of happiness between children, husband
and wife

Then somehow things change though out all the years
When the days and nights of love slowly turn to tears

In life it seems that this happens in love all too many
times
When what was once the light of your life no longer
shines

So you can accept what is happening and let it go
astray
Or you can fight to save your love before it fades
away

Just Getting By

While going through a little town just the other day
I saw an old man carrying a garbage bag shuffling
along the way

There was no doubt by the way he looked his life was
not much fun
He was wearing dirty ragged clothes carrying his
possessions in the sun

This started me thinking about where his life went
wrong
Family problems or mental illness that had been
going on to long

Was this man a business man or a forgotten veteran of
war
And is he doomed to live life this way from now to
evermore

I have been through hard times just like most of you
But I knew I had family there to always get me
through

I know I will never go hungry or have a roof over my
head
I will never have to dig in garbage to find old food or
bread

It's hard to imagine what went wrong in his life or
why
But as so many out there he lives life just getting by

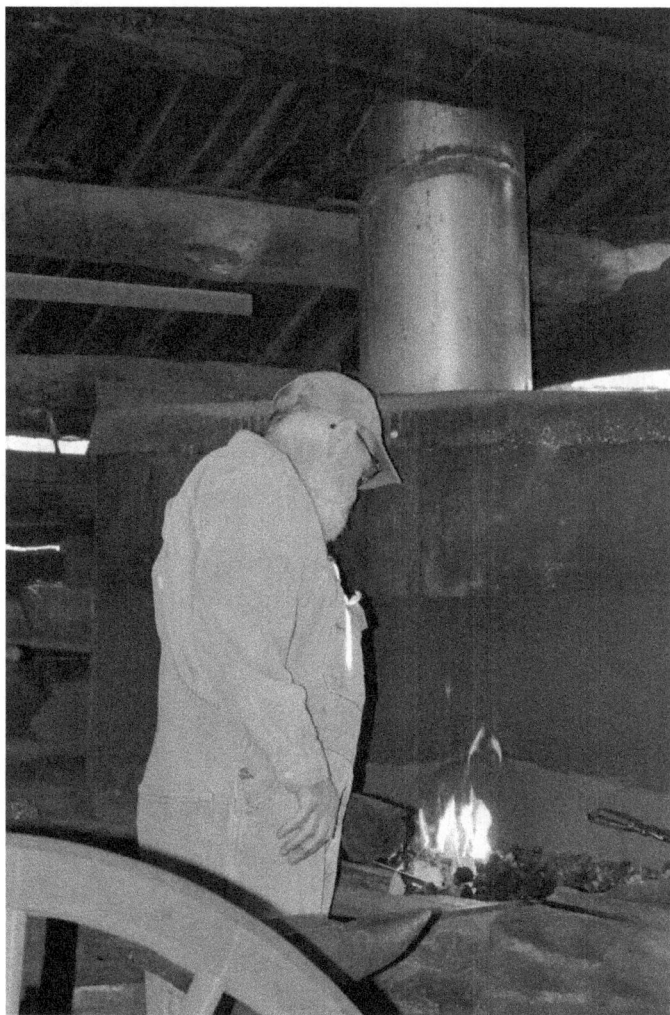

Calluses and Dirty Hands

From the day you are born your parents preach every
day
They tell you being a Doctor or Lawyer is the best
way

They say go to college and get your degree
Your life will be good this you will see

But when we look around there are so many paths
Thank goodness college wasn't in everyone's past

When you look around this country at everything you
see
You see schools, bridges and houses built for you and
me

As you sit at the table and enjoy tonight's meal
Just give a short thought to the farmer in the field

When you leave home in your car to drive your child
to school
Remember your car wasn't built by a Doctor but by a
man with tools

Some people look down at workers with hands
covered with grease
But you need to remember without them progress
would cease

continued

These hard workers build, farm and are the backbone of our land
So I thank God for the man with calluses and dirt on their hands

Mabry Mill

The old cedar shingles are weathered from the storms
The old grey wood lap siding is all buckled and worn

The water wheel is still turning with water from
upstream
The trees and grass at the mill are all so lush and so
green

As I sit here on the side of this old Virginia country
road
And think back through times that were here so long
ago

How hard these people worked and the struggles and
strife
All they ever wanted was to provide their children a
better life

I'm sure as they worked all day grinding the grits
from grain
The thought of erasing history never even entered
their brain

Monuments of this Appalachian life surely needs to
be preserved
Like all other monuments of our history that our
children sure deserve

Continued

If we destroy all things that reflect our past at the whim of one's will
Our children will never enjoy a moment like this sitting at Mabry Mill

Little Towns Die

I love to drive the back roads throughout this
land
But there is one thing I notice time and time
again

Every small town is full of the stores that are
closed
There are no longer small stores to buy shoes
and clothes

The bicycle shop and lunch counter are no
longer there
Just empty buildings with broken glass
everywhere

The new four lane highway was built around
this small town
Then after this happens these small stores were
left to drown

Kids no longer ride bikes Saturday downtown to
the show
They have no reason to even go to town
anymore you know

continued

Everything is bought online or out at the new
big box store
Walking on the towns crowded streets will
happen no more

As I slowly drove around this deserted little
town I wanted to cry
Because so much is lost when we let these little
towns die

The Lonely Trucker

As we travel down the highway we see them
everyday
Sometimes we flash our lights to move them out of
the way

These are the truckers than move everything we need
to buy
And without these tireless heroes of the road we
could not get by

Everything we eat or drink and on the bed at night we
lie
At some point it was on a truck traveling through the
night

The trucker is always away from their family and
their friends
Hauling everything we need from our food to a
Mercedes Benz

They travel through the rain and snow seven days a
week
They have to deliver their load on time sometimes
with little sleep

- continued

While most of us go home at 5 eat and then sit down
and relax
The truckers are waiting to get loaded for the that
long haul going back

Christmas Day while you're at home with your
spouse and your kids
Some lonely trucker is behind the wheel wishing he
was home with his

Lawmakers That Really Care

We The People elect our lawmakers to represent what
we need
To pass legislation that will make our lives better and
take the lead

But something always seems to happen when once
they gain their power
And they take their place at the capital at their office
in their ivory tower

The driving force of their decisions is no longer for
you and me
But for lobbyist and power brokers that give the
money they need

They have no concern over border safety and our
medical care
As long as when the next election comes they win and
remain there

So when you watch the news tonight and see them
telling their lies
Just keep in mind the only end to this will be when
term limits arrive

Continued

The system is in a sad state and the only way to repair what's happening there
Is with term limits that will get rid of the crooks and create Lawmakers that really care

Wow I finally ran out of brilliant things to say.

Hope Ya'll enjoyed my little life observations and hopefully you read something that hit home for you.

Keep an eye out for Volume 2!!

www.ingramcontent.com/pod-product-compliance
Lightning Source LLC
Chambersburg PA
CBHW070527030426
42337CB00016B/2142